Living
Kenya

Ruth Thomson

Photography by David Hampton

W
FRANKLIN WATTS
LONDON•SYDNEY

First published in 2002 by
Franklin Watts,
338 Euston Road
London NW1 3BH

Franklin Watts Australia
Level 17/207 Kent Street, Sydney, NSW 2000

Series editor: Ruth Thomson
Series designer: Edward Kinsey
Consultant: Rob Bowden
(EASI-Educational resourcing)
Additional photographs:
Ashley Cameron page 24(l), 29(l)

A CIP catalogue record for this book is
available from the British Library.
Dewey Classification 916.76

ISBN 978 0 7496 6345 2
Printed in China

Franklin Watts is a division of Hachette
Children's Books, an Hachette Livre UK
company.

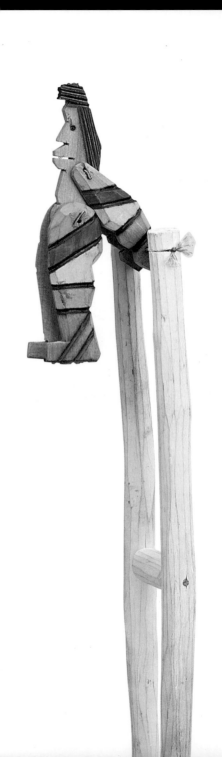

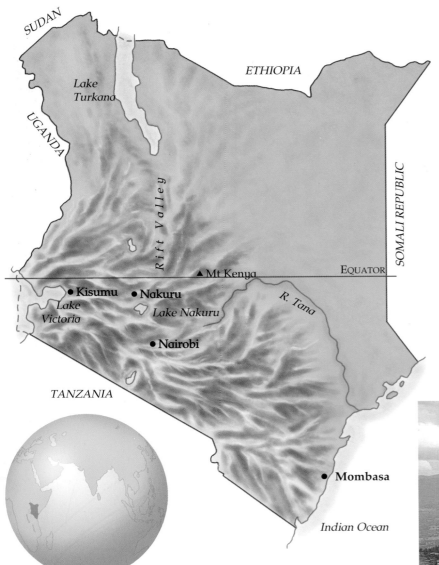

◁ **Picking tea**
Tea plantations cover the wet, fertile slopes of the highlands near Lake Victoria. Tea is one of Kenya's most important cash crops.

▷**The Rift Valley**
This enormous valley runs right through Kenya from north to south. It is dotted with lakes and volcanoes.

Nairobi – the capital

Nairobi started in 1899 as a depot and repair camp for workers building the railway across the country. It quickly grew into a large town and became the capital. It is now the biggest and most important city in the country.

△**The Uhuru Garden monument**
Kenya was once a British colony. This sculpture of Kenyans raising their national flag celebrates their independence from the British in 1963.

△**Walking crowds**
Over two million people live in Nairobi. Those who live in the shanty towns walk into the centre to work.

◁**The city centre**
Central Nairobi has some smart shops, restaurants and cinemas, as well as Parliament buildings, museums and a conference centre.

▷**All Saints' Cathedral**
Most Kenyans are Christian. The country's main cathedral was built by the British.

◁▽**A city of contrasts**
The city centre has many modern offices and hotels. Nearby are the shanty towns where over half the people of Nairobi live.

▽**Modern facilities**
There are several new shopping malls and an increasing number of internet cafes. These are used mainly by the well-off.

Famous sights

The most memorable trip for most visitors to Kenya is a safari to one of its national parks. Mammals, such as wildebeest, giraffes, cheetahs, zebra, antelopes, warthogs and the 'Big Five', roam freely in these protected places.

Some parks have spectacular landscapes, including swamps, gorges, mountains, lakes, geysers or hot springs.

△**Fort Jesus, Mombasa**
This is one of Kenya's most important historical sights. It was built as a stronghold in 1593, but is now a museum.

▷**Nairobi National Park**
The oldest national park in the country is outside Nairobi. Kenyans, especially school children, visit this as much as tourists.

△**The Big Five**
Tourists who go on safari always hope to spot the Big Five – lion, buffalo, elephant, leopard and rhino.

A brochure for one of the national parks

NAIROBI SAFARI WALK

△▽Craft souvenirs
The craft market in Nairobi sells carvings, baskets and other souvenirs from all over Kenya.

△A paradise for birds
Almost 400 species of birds can be found at Lake Nakuru. More than a million flamingos feed in the shallows.

Living in towns and cities

Fewer than a third of Kenyans live in towns or cities. However, city populations are growing steadily year by year. The biggest cities are Nairobi and the port of Mombasa. These have great extremes of wealth and poverty.

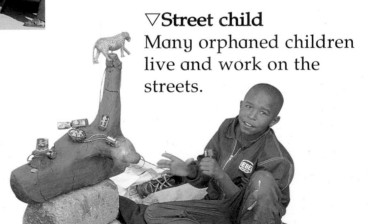

◁Public transport
Auto rickshaws carry one or two passengers. *Matatus*, privately owned minibuses, can take up to 20 people at a time.

Auto rickshaws

△Housing
The better off live in concrete houses or flats with tiled roofs. The poor live in mud shacks with corrugated iron roofs. These have no running water or electricity.

Matatus

▽Street child
Many orphaned children live and work on the streets.

◁▷Street traders

Shoe makers, food stalls and other street sellers have their own regular spots on the pavements.

Sandals made from recycled tyres

▷Office workers

Well-educated people can find office work in banks, businesses and the government.

People at work

Most city workers work for themselves. Some work in small street workshops, making furniture, shoes, clothes or metal utensils. Others sell food or goods or offer a service, such as shoe cleaning or haircutting. Large numbers of people have no work at all.

Living in the country

Away from the towns, people live in small settlements scattered across the countryside.

In most places, they live in traditional mud huts with thatched roofs. Elsewhere, people have mud or concrete homes with corrugated iron roofs.

△**The post office**
Villagers go to the nearest post office to collect mail. Letters are put into individual, locked letterboxes.

△**A village street**
Many villages consist of a single, unpaved street. They have a few shops (*dukas*) that stock household basics.

▷**A traditional house**
The pointed, thatched roof keeps a mud house cool and dry.

12

◁ **Left to dry**
Wet washing is laid over bushes, where it dries quickly. Ironing is done using an iron filled with hot charcoal.

▽**On foot**
Cars are rare in the countryside. Women may walk a long way with their shopping on their heads.

△**Washing clothes**
In places without running water, it is far easier to wash clothes in the river than to bring enough water home for the job.

Working in the country

Four out of five Kenyans work on the land, growing crops either for themselves or to sell. They live mainly in the west or south, where the soil is fertile and there is enough rainfall to water the crops.

Most families own land, called a *shamba*, where they grow their food. They may also keep cows, goats and sheep for milk or meat.

△**Farming**
Many people use iron hoes to dig the ground. Very few farmers can afford a tractor.

Shamba crops

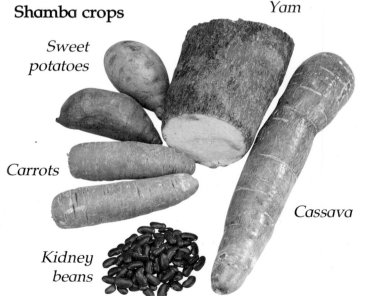

Yam

Sweet potatoes

Carrots

Cassava

Kidney beans

△**Carving wood**
In places which suffer from drought, it is hard to grow crops. Some people earn money to buy food by making wood-carvings for tourists.

◁Coffee picking
Coffee beans grow in the cool, wet highlands. They are picked in December and laid out on long tables to dry in the sun.

Freshly-picked coffee beans

▽Fresh today
These fresh fruits and vegetables are grown for foreign markets and flown abroad every day.

Cash crops
Crops grown to sell abroad provide nearly half of the country's wealth. Kenya produces a tenth of the world's tea. Other important cash crops are coffee, peas, French beans, sugar cane and cut flowers, especially roses.

Mango

Pineapple

Mange-touts

Guava

French beans

Passion fruit

Aubergines

15

Fuel and water

In most rural areas, houses have no electricity supply, running water or flush toilets. Women and children have to collect the firewood and water. These are tiring, time-consuming tasks.

△**Collecting firewood**
Children collect fallen branches as fuel for cooking. They look for specific types which do not make too much smoke when they burn.

▷**A charcoal store**
Some people buy charcoal for their cooking stoves (*jiko*).

△**Paraffin lamps**
Villagers use paraffin lamps, candles or torches to light their homes.

Matches

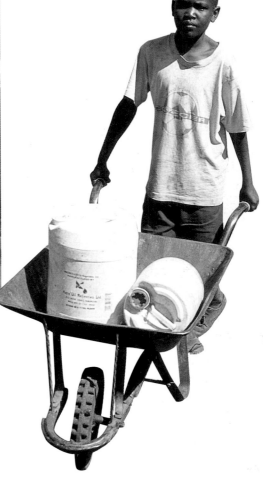

Water supplies

There are two main seasons in Kenya – rainy and dry. However, in the north, water is often scarce and there is a constant threat of drought.

Usually, people collect water from rivers. Sometimes these are polluted and can cause illness.

△Buying water

During the dry season, there is often a water shortage. Some people have to buy water from a water tanker. They store it in plastic containers.

▷Bottled water

Those who can afford it can buy bottled water for drinking. This is safer than river water.

△Collecting water

With a wheelbarrow, children can transport a good quantity of water at a time.

17

Shopping

Most towns have a weekly market which attracts people from all around. People buy food from women who come to sell the surplus from their *shambas*, as well as from professional traders.

People often buy clothes, shoes and furniture directly from their makers – tailors, shoemakers and carpenters.

△General shop
Villages often have a general shop where people can buy drinks, packet food, fruit and small household goods.

▷Going to market
Markets are held outdoors. As well as food, traders may sell cooking pots, crockery, brushes and second-hand clothes.

△Live chickens
Sometimes people stand by the roadside, hoping to sell their live chickens to passers-by.

▷Food measuring

Dry foods are sold by volume, rather than by weight. Amounts are measured by tinfuls.

Some packaged goods

An ironmonger's shop

Packaging

Very few foods or goods are sold pre-packed. Dry goods are sold from large sacks; meat is cut fresh at the butcher's. Glass and plastic bottles are recycled.

Only factory goods, such as flour, detergent and margarine, come in packets or tins.

A butcher's shop

On the move

▷Trains

The main railway runs between Nairobi and Mombasa. Trains are no longer an important form of transport. They are slow and expensive.

Very few Kenyans can afford to buy a car. Most people walk or cycle locally. They travel to the nearest market by *matatu*. People get on and off these minibuses anywhere they like along the route. They use larger buses for longer journeys.

▽▷Tough bicycles

Bikes have two cross-bars and covered chains for cycling on bumpy roads. Many villages have repair workshops (*fundi*) for mending the frequent punctures.

△Country roads

In rural areas, roads are often made of packed earth. These are dusty in the dry season and muddy in the rainy season.

△Ferries
This car ferry travels
between Mombasa
island and the coast.

▽Transporting goods
Lorries carry goods
along the Trans-Africa
highway from Mombasa
into Central Africa.

△Long-distance buses
Regular buses travel between
major towns. They stop at bus
stations along the way.

△Donkeys
Donkeys are used in the country
to carry crops, firewood and water.

The roads

The main roads between towns are
tarmac, but are often full of potholes.
Since they are not always regularly
repaired, there are often accidents.

Family life

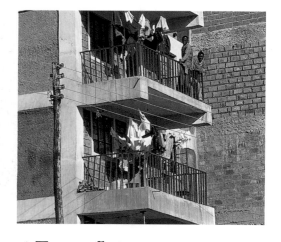

△**Town flats**
In towns, many families live in small, crowded flats.

▽**A compound**
A compound is often built in a circular shape, like this.

City families live in houses or flats. In the country, many families live together with their relatives in a compound. This is a collection of several houses, one for each family unit.

These extended families share the separate kitchen and the storehouses for maize and beans. There is also a pen for keeping animals safe at night. As a family grows in size, new houses may be added to the compound.

△Cooking
Women do all the cooking on an open fire or use a charcoal stove (*jiko*).

▽Eating together
Families share their meal around a small, low table. They use enamel crockery.

▷Boys' jobs
After school, boys help fetch water or look after the farm animals.

▽Girls' jobs
Girls often look after a smaller brother or sister. They also sweep and often wash up.

23

Time to eat

Millions of Kenyans do not have enough to eat every day. Cheap and filling dishes are made from maize, sweet potatoes and kidney beans. They are often served with a meat sauce. Almost everyone drinks sweet, milky tea (*chai*).

△Breakfast

For breakfast, people usually have a bowl of *uji*. This thin porridge is made from maize flour, mixed with sugar and milk.

▷Barbecued meat

People enjoy having barbecued meat (*nyama choma*) at eating places like this one.

△A wealth of fruit

The varied climate means that fruit is available all year round. At different seasons there are bananas, passion fruit, pineapple, oranges and watermelons.

◁Preserving food

Very few housholds have a fridge, so fish and meat are often preserved to stop them from going rotten.

▷Roast maize

Roadside sellers roast maize on a grill for people to buy as a snack.

▽Using maize

Maize can be dried easily and stored for a long time. It is ground into meal, which is mixed with water and cooked. This sets hard into a dish called *ugali*.

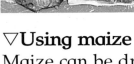

Maize meal

Ugali

25

School time

Children can go to primary school for eight years. The government pays for the teachers, but parents often have to raise money for the upkeep and repairs of the school buildings.

Since not every family can afford the school uniform and books, not every child in Kenya goes to school.

△**Going to school**
Country children walk to school. It may take some an hour or more.

▷**Lessons**
Pupils learn practical subjects, including agriculture, carpentry and domestic science, as well as maths, Kiswahili, English and science.

△**School facilities**
Most classrooms are in single storey blocks. There are separate toilet and washing facilities. There is usually a playing field for games and school assemblies.

26

◁Farming lessons

Rural schools have their own vegetable garden (*shamba*), where pupils work. The produce is sold to raise money for the school.

▷Higher education

Kenya has several universities. The biggest, in Nairobi, has 20,000 students.

Ruler

Kiswahili book

Pencil

Pencil sharpener

English book

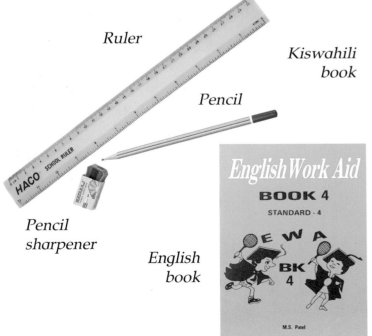

Exercise book

Kiswahili reading books

Having fun

Many Kenyans have very little time for leisure. In the country, there is always work to be done. Few people have money to spare for luxuries. During their spare time, many women make crafts, such as baskets, mats or jewellery, for their own use.

▽**Playing football**
Children make footballs from plastic bags tightly wound together with string or rubber bands.

△**Football shirts for sale**
Many people support English football teams. Owning an imported second-hand football shirt is much prized.

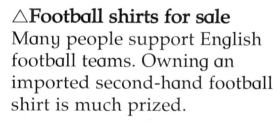

▽**Time for a snack**
In cities, a favourite treat is a bottle of pop and a packet of crisps.

◁Radio
Radio broadcasts are
mainly in Kiswahili
or English.

▷Home-made toys
Children recycle wire,
scrap tin, wood, string
and fabric to make
toys that move.

Wire toy

Time to tune in
Millions of households have battery
radios. People listen to the national
network, or to local stations which play
African and Western pop music.
Television is rare, except in the big cities.

Going further

Kenyan fruit and vegetables

Look at the fruit and vegetables in a supermarket to discover which come from Kenya.

Make a list of the foods and their cost per kilo. Add some locally produced foods to your list and compare their cost with the Kenyan ones.

Make a wire model

Use some soft wire to make a toy model. You may like to make a bike or a car, as Kenyan children do, or you may prefer to make a spaceship or an aeroplane. You could also make a person or a building.

Leave the model plain or cover it with strips of scrap fabric.

Make a safari guide

Find out more about some of the animals you might see in a Kenyan national park.

Make a safari guide, using a piece of paper folded into three. Draw some pictures of the animals or stick down some photographs cut out from colour magazines or holiday brochures. Write a short caption about each animal.

Websites

http://kenyaweb.com

http://yahooligans.yahoo.com/reference/factbook/ke/index.html

Glossary

Cash crop A crop that is grown for sale and not as food for the farmer.

Colony A country that is ruled by people from another country.

Currency The money used by a country.

Drought A long period where there is very little rainfall or none at all.

Equator The imaginary line around the widest part of the Earth, which is an equal distance from the North and South poles.

Fertile Able to produce a plentiful supply.

Independence The time when a country begins to rule itself, after being ruled by another one.

Geyser A spring that spouts hot water into the air.

Mangroves Trees that grow in muddy swamps on tropical coasts or riverbanks. Their long roots grow above the ground.

Plain An area of flat land.

Plantation Land planted with a single crop, such as tea, coffee or rubber.

Polluted Dirty and harmful to people, animals and plants.

Population The total number of people living in a place.

Safari A journey, often in search of wild animals.

Shanty town Unplanned city housing with no power, water supply, sewers or rubbish collection.

Staple The food that people eat every day.

Spring The place where an underground stream comes out to the surface.

Volcano A cone-shaped mountain lying over an underground chamber of molten rock. Sometimes pressure from hot gases causes a volcano to erupt.

Index